THE FIRE IN THE WOOD

ALSO BY PETER THABIT JONES

Poetry

Tacky Brow (Outposts Publications, UK, 1974)
The Apprenticeship (Cwm Nedd Press, UK, 1977)
Clocks Tick Differently (Celtion Poetry Series, UK, 1980)
Visitors (Poetry Wales Press, UK, 1986)
The Cold Cold Corner (Dark Lane Poetry, UK, 1995)
Ballad of Kilvey Hill (Swansea Bay Publishers/Eastside Poetry, UK, 1999)
The Lizard Catchers (Cross-Cultural Communications, USA, 2006 /reprinted 2007 & 2008)
POET TO POET #1: Bridging the Waters: Swansea to Sag Harbor, with American poet Vince Clemente (Cross-Cultural Communications, USA, and The Seventh Quarry Press, UK, 2008)
Whispers of the Soul, with American poet Vince Clemente (a bilingual collection: English/Romanian). Translated by Dr. Olimpia Iacob (Editura Fundatiei Poezia Iasi, Romania, 2008)
The Boy and the Lion's Head (a verse drama, bilingual: English/Romanian). Translated by Dr. Olimpia Iacob (Citadela Publishing, Romania, 2009)
Poems from a Cabin on Big Sur (Cross-Cultural Communications, USA, 2011)
Where the Butterflies Go/Songs for a Dark Bird (Two bilingual collections of poems in one book. Romania's Aura Cristi's *Where the Butterflies Go*/Peter's *Songs for a Dark Bird*. Translated by Dr. Olimpia Iacob and Jim Kacian (Timpul Publishing, Romania, 2014)
Selected Poems (bilingual collection: English/Romanian). Translated by Dr. Monica Manolachi of the University of Bucharest. (Bibliotecha Universalis/Collectiile Revistei 'Orizont Literar Contemporan', 2016)

Prose

Dylan Thomas Walking Tour of Greenwich Village, New York, with Aeronwy Thomas (for the Wales International Centre, New York/Welsh Assembly Government, 2008, PDF www.walesworldnation.com) PODCAST: www.dylanthomaswalkingtourmp3.com

Dylan Thomas Walking Tour of Greenwich Village, New York tourist pocket book, with Aeronwy Thomas (Cross-Cultural Communications, USA, and The Seventh Quarry Press, UK, 2014)

Dylan Thomas Walking Tour of Greenwich Village, New York smartphone app, with Aeronwy Thomas (DT100/Dylan Thomas Centenary, Welsh Government, Literature Wales, and The British Council, 2014)

DVDs

Walking with Dylan Thomas/documentary film based on the *Dylan Thomas Walking Tour of Greenwich Village* (Cross-Cultural Communications, USA, and The Seventh Quarry Press, UK, 2010)

The Poet, the Hunchback, and the Boy/drama (Dylan Thomas Theatre, Holly Tree Productions, and The Seventh Quarry Press, 2014)

Peter Thabit Jones

THE FIRE IN THE WOOD

A prose and verse drama

Three Acts based on the life of Edmund Kara
California's Big Sur sculptor

Cross-Cultural Communications
New York, USA

The Seventh Quarry Press,
Swansea, Wales, UK
2017

Copyright © 2017 by Peter Thabit Jones
Copyright © 2017 Foreword by Patricia Holt
Copyright © 2017 Foreword quotation from An Embryo Emerging
by Carolyn Mary Kleefeld
Copyright © 2017 Photo of Phoenix by John Dotson
Copyright © 2017 Texts by Carolyn Mary Kleefeld:
Artist neighbour on the mountain speech: pages 2/3; Artist neighbour on the mountain speech: pages 30/31/32; Within the Robes of Friendship poem: page 34
Copyright © 2017 Supplement Photos by Peter Thabit Jones and Patricia Holt
Copyright © 2017 Supplement Drawings by Carolyn Mary Kleefeld
Copyright © 2017 Photo of Edmund Kara at work by Walter Chappell

All rights reserved under International Copyright Conventions. Except for brief passages quoted in a newspaper, magazine, or television or Internet review, no part of this book may be reproduced in any form or by any means electronic or mechanical, including photocopying and recording or by any information storage and retrieval system, without permission in writing from the publishers or the authors.

Cross-Cultural Communications
239 Wynsum Avenue
Merrick, New York 11566-4725 USA
Tel: (516) 868-5635 / Fax: (516) 379-1901
cccpoetry@aol.com
www.cross-culturalcommunications.com

The Seventh Quarry Press
8 Cherry Crescent
Swansea SA4 9FG Wales, UK
Tel: (UK) 07964039928
info@peterthabitjones.com
www.peterthabitjones.com

Library of Congress Control Number: 2016958232
ISBN 978-0-89304-358-2
Front and back cover photos by Peter Thabit Jones

First Edition
Printed in Wales by Dinefwr Print & Design, Llandybie, Carmarthenshire, Wales, UK

ACKNOWLEDGMENTS

Carolyn Mary Kleefeld, poet and artist, for the use of several of her texts and paintings (please see copyright page).

Glen Cheda, Edmund Kara's benefactor, for the valuable materials and photos he gave me whilst I was doing research on Edmund's life and for his ongoing encouragement.

David Jay Brown, writer, for his very informative and most helpful interview with Edmund Kara on March 29th, 1996, which is on Edmund Kara's website.

Rick Deragon, writer, for his article on Edmund Kara, published September 3rd, 1990, California.

David Cushing Fuess, writer, for his article, *Art and the Artist*, on Edmund Kara (date of article unknown).

www.edmundkara.com

IN MEMORY OF EDMUND KARA

Special thanks to Carolyn Mary Kleefeld, artist and poet, for the writer-in-residence time in her Big Sur cabin, from May to July 2012, which allowed the writing of the drama, and for her very informative chats and constant and enthusiastic encouragement.

Many thanks to Patricia Holt for writing her much appreciated Foreword for this book and for her constant and enthusiastic encouragement.

Thanks to John Dotson who first introduced me to the Big Sur area when he booked Aeronwy Thomas and me for a West Coast event, which was part of Aeronwy's and my six weeks tour of America, the 2008 Dylan Thomas Tribute Tour, organized by Stanley H. Barkan of Cross-Cultural Communications, New York.

Thanks to John Larson and Laura Zabrowski for the many kindnesses during my residency.

Thanks to all my other dear Big Sur friends.

Lastly, my gratitude to my New York mentor Vince Clemente, poet and critic, and my American publisher Stanley H. Barkan, also a poet, for their constant support and encouragement over the years.

CONTENTS

Foreword 13

Introduction 15

The Fire in the Wood 17

Photos and Drawings Supplement 67

About the Author 85

Some comments on other books by Peter Thabit Jones 89

FOREWORD

In "The Fire in the Wood" Peter masterfully manifests the power of Edmund Kara's art, sculptures, and life. We sense viscerally the unrelenting vision, the stunning wild terrain, the raw, sensuous act of sculpting, the elemental, yet refined expression.

We do not watch or read the drama; we are not observers. Rather, through Peter's own art, we inhabit Edmund and experience his life drama from within him. His ever-expansive embrace of life, which he transformed into his art, his fidelity to the pure instinct of creation, his passions come alive too within us.

To create in this manner, Peter draws on his own commanding skill and talent to humble himself fearlessly, allowing the presence of Edmund to speak directly to him and to be a catalyst and guide to that well of mystery, a unity before separation, where all true art is created. This source from which Edmund created his sculptures, Peter accesses to create his drama.

And so, the poet and playwright from Swansea conveys the essence of the sculptor from New York, LA, and ultimately Big Sur, although they never actually met. Bringing us "The Ghost of Old Edmund Kara," "Young Edmund Kara," "The Bird Dancer," "The Neighbor on the Mountain," and a sort of Greek chorus of others, and juxtaposing poetry, prose, visual art, music, dance, as well as the haunting sounds of wind and sea, Peter recreates a full measure of Edmund's life.

Yet too, although the drama is a gripping rendition of one particular man's life, it is also a paean to creativity, with Edmund a powerful archetype for the creative process itself.

This creative calling is expressed poignantly by Edmund's beloved friend and neighbor, Big Sur poet and artist, Carolyn Mary Kleefeld, in these stanzas from her poem, "An Embryo Emerging,"

> ". . . In a time wrought with anguish,
> when the sun is denied
> and the stars become infidels,
> she is reborn.
>
> Is this what it takes to be a poet?
> Is this a madness
> the gods confer upon the innocent? . . ."

Indeed, in his drama, Peter elicits such questioning, portraying multitudinous aspects of a creative life—from a sense of "the heartbreak at the heart of things" (from John Hall Wheelock and often quoted to Peter by his cherished friend and mentor, Vince Clemente) driving much creativity, to a need for personal expression which withstands market considerations and the lure of fame, to solitude, to endurance, to vision, and beyond. Through these explorations, Peter guides the drama from the personal to the universal.

The "Young Edmund Kara" says, "Wood is my tongue." Words are Peter's tongue, and sculpting with words as exquisitely as Edmund did with wood, the poet evokes the sculptor, together creating this work of art.

Patricia Holt
Longtime friend and neighbor of Edmund Kara

Big Sur, California
November 2016

INTRODUCTION

Edmund Kara (1925–2001) spent a creative and isolated life in a cabin and studio lodged rather precariously on a cliff overlooking the Pacific Ocean. He spent almost forty years in Big Sur, California, meticulously carving his amazing sculptures, whilst shunning the art world, its trends, and exhibitions.

His "Phoenix Bird", on display outside Big Sur's Nepenthe Restaurant, off Highway 1, has been seen by visitors from around the world; and his nude sculpture of Elizabeth Taylor, used in the Vincente Minnelli-directed film *The Sandpiper*, which also starred Welshman Richard Burton, gained Kara much attention in Hollywood and Europe. He did do some commissions, including sculptured doors for film-star legend Clint Eastwood.

Prior to his reclusive lifestyle in Big Sur, he had worked as a costume designer in New York and Los Angeles; and he designed for the likes of jazz legend and film star Lena Horne and singer Peggy Lee. He also worked for Paramount Studios and Universal Studios in Los Angeles.

This three-act drama utilises poetry, prose, music, photos, film, and several paintings and several texts by Big Sur's international artist and poet Carolyn Mary Kleefeld, who was a close friend of Edmund Kara, to evoke aspects of his remarkable life.

Peter Thabit Jones

The Phoenix sculpture
© 2017 John Dotson

CHARACTERS

The Ghost of Old Edmund Kara (an elderly, white-bearded man who looks physically strong and confident)

Young Edmund Kara (a man in his late thirties, dark-bearded, physically strong and confident)

Dinka Kara (silhouette only)

Voice of Poet 1 (male)

Voice of Poet 2 (female)

Artist Neighbour on the Mountain (a woman with long dark hair, wearing a bright-red flowing dressing-gown)

Two Female Fashion Models

The Bird Dancer (a male dancer dressed in a bird-like outfit of long black and blood-red feathers)

Nepenthe Restaurant Customers (at least six people)

ACT ONE

Scene 1

The curtain is lifted to a stage of fog. After a few moments, in chorus, slow and controlled.

VOICES OF POETS 1 and 2:

Fog
Is a slow
And steady
Ghost,
Leaving
Its breath
Of dawn
Over
An unseen
Paradise.

Fog
Veils the eyes
Of the cabin
With graveyard
Silence,
And smokes
The long
And
Blurred-stroked
Moments.

Fog
Is a slow
And heavy cloud,
An old man's
Quilt
Pulled over
The ocean.

Fog
Is a strange
And lovely death,
Whose cold shroud
Brings in (*slightly louder*)
One man's
Story.

The loud sounds of the ocean and the wind. **THE GHOST OF OLD EDMUND KARA**, *dressed in a black tee-shirt, black trousers, and black shoes, comes out of the fog. The fog lifts, to reveal (ideally) a replica (or back-drop photo or film) of his derelict cabin. As he speaks, the photo changes to other photos of his cabin (or the film just continues). The sounds of the ocean and the wind go down in volume, but are still important to the overall atmosphere.*

THE GHOST OF OLD EDMUND KARA: Am I the ghost of this cabin or is this cabin the ghost of me? (*He moves forward*). Who am I anyway? Or should that be who was I? (*Emphasising*) No, I'll stick with the present. I am Edmund Kara—and this is my derelict cabin.

A woman, with long dark hair and wearing a bright-red flowing dressing-gown, enters the stage on the right. He does not look at her.

ARTIST NEIGHBOUR ON THE MOUNTAIN (*tenderly*): Edmund, your cabin, the lair where you once dwelled, has become a living testament to your life. How fitting that this external womb where you created your masterful sculptures is gradually sliding from the cliffs to the sea below. Your Zen way of living is now being exhibited like a final living sculpture, in cadence with Nature's rhythms, the vast Mystery that moves what remains of your existence back to the primal waters. (*Pause*)

On the eroding, earthen driveway are keep-out signs and gates, yet death and its guests cannot be blocked. Rats and other trespassers leave their dung in what once was your impressive gallery, your cave of invention. The tall, narrow cabin windows, shattered by Nature's forces into kaleidoscopic fragments, are now open to the sea's thrust. Swallows fly frantically in and out, building their nests in the old wooden rafters. And the once impeccable, yet indigenous gardens, released from your concepts of beauty grow freely in their own wild season. (*Pause*)

Where we used to lie long ago on sofas opposite each other, the rats now have parties. And through the planks in the floor, I see the jutting cliffs below. The heater, refrigerator, and propane tank have tumbled down to the water's edge. The wooden deck just above the sea where we once enjoyed our tea-sipping communes continues its fall into aquatic oblivion. (*Pause*)

Yes, beloved Edmund, only the present moment is real. The rest is breaking open to a yet untold history, the Blazing Eternal.

She exits the stage.

THE GHOST OF OLD EDMUND KARA: My creative shell (*emphasising*) and my creative hell! But, ah, the obvious questions that most of you must be thinking. Did the Pacific Ocean drive me mad? The eternal workings of its constant roaring. The luscious lap-lapping of the enormous crash of its waves. And what of the lament of the wind, weathering its wild sadness all around the cabin, wailing its grief in and out of my head?

Was I already mad to move to such an island of a place and build a cliff-edge nest for myself and my creations? Did the loneliness crowd in and gnaw away at my thoughts?

(*Assured*) No, I was young enough, confident, definitely arrogant, and more than ready to live like a bloody monk.

He looks to the left and to the right. He turns to look at the backdrop and then faces the audience again.

THE GHOST OF OLD EDMUND KARA (*tongue-in-cheek*): They say you can see the essence of a person in their home. (*He laughs*). So who was the (*emphasising*) real Edmund Kara. The recluse of a sculptor in this cabin on the rim of the Pacific Ocean for almost forty years, or the costume designer lording it up with the kings and the queens of New York and Los Angeles?

He moves forward and sighs deeply.

THE GHOST OF OLD EDMUND KARA: Ah, where do I start? With the cabin which I designed and built? Big Sur and the life-force of the Pacific Ocean? Hollywood? Liz Taylor and Richard Burton and THE SANDPIPER film? Nepenthe and my now famous Phoenix Bird sculpture? And what about a sculptor's life? (*Pause*) Let's start with me. (*Proudly and grandly*) I am Edmund Kara.

The lights dim until there is just a spotlight on **THE GHOST OF OLD EDMUND KARA**. *The sounds of the ocean and the wind stop. Then the sound of a shrieking bird is heard.*

THE GHOST OF OLD EDMUND KARA: I entered the world (*mischievously*) as flesh and bone, of course, in 1925 in New Jersey. (*Pause*) October 17th. (*Pause*) I was one of five children, three girls and two boys, and fatherless—he died when I was four. A blur of a few memories of him is all I have. A Jewish baby, the grandson of immigrants from Eastern Europe, I was the youngest son.

My mother, Anna, owned a grocery store and I helped her all I could. The hive-buzz of my sisters busied itself through my world day in, day out. But I was a bird in the wrong nest, a lone bird waiting to find its own part of the sky.

I believe I was born to create, born with hands (*he holds out his hands dramatically*) that would reveal my unquiet heart. As a boy, I watched my mother and sisters sew, as diligent as bees at work and I took to the slow and patient craft of it. Creativity began to ooze out of me. Aged twelve, I had a show of my portraits at the public library in Roselle, New Jersey. *(Pause)* I was *(emphasising)* <u>so</u> curious about people then. *(Pause)*

A young man, *(he chuckles)* around the age of seventeen, I began working in New York, the cloud-touching metropolis, the bustling concrete sculpture of streets and skyscrapers. I got a job at Macy's, in the display department. I loved drawing and I got hooked on the idea of designing clothes. It led to working in fashion design and fashion illustration for advertising agencies. *(Pause)*

I had studied at the Arts High School in New Jersey, so I carried a sense of formal training with me. *(Pause)* Some friends connected me with Lena Horne, the jazz singer and movie star at MGM. For three years I designed what she wore in her performances. She, an incredibly beautiful woman, was the living mannequin of my mind's creations. The working-class boy from Roselle Park, New Jersey, had arrived.

The spotlight goes out. **THE GHOST OF OLD EDMUND KARA** *exits the stage. Then we hear very lively and up tempo jazz music. Coloured swathes of light wash the stage quickly. The jazz music gets louder. A photo of New York skyscrapers fills the backdrop.*

VOICE OF POET 1 *(shouting like a newspaper seller and clear above the music):* New York! New York! New York! New York!

The coloured swathes of light stop and the music goes down in volume. We see a lit-up white backdrop. Behind the backdrop, we see the silhouette of **YOUNG EDMUND KARA** *working at a desk, drawing, and the silhouette of his sister, Dinka, sat and working at a sewing machine. As* **THE GHOST OF OLD EDMUND KARA** *comes on to the right of the stage, the music goes up in volume.*

THE GHOST OF OLD EDMUND KARA *(loudly):* I designed high-fashion dresses, under my own label, for an elegant dress shop in the city that never sleeps. My younger sister, Diana, whom we called Dinka, and I laboured away in our workshop, which was financed by my dear mother, Anna. We laboured away the precious hours of our young lives.

Two female fashion models strut on to the stage, gaggling like geese (talking nonsense), and strut around **THE GHOST OF OLD EDMUND KARA.**

The loud sound of a money till.

VOICE OF POET 2 *(happily and gratefully, like a shop assistant):* Thank you, madam! *(Emphasising)* <u>Thank</u> you!

The two female fashion models exit (in the same manner as they entered).

The backdrop darkens and the music stops. The light dims until there is just a spotlight on **THE GHOST OF OLD EDMUND KARA**, *who has moved to centre stage.*

THE GHOST OF OLD EDMUND KARA: Running my own business was not for me! I did not like the competitive world. I didn't like the responsibility of the day-to-day being chained to a repetitive experience, and dealing with all the business aspects. *(Pause)* Around the age of twenty-three, I began a trip around the world, much of it by bicycle. I first crossed America, lodging in very cheap places. I cycled up to eighty miles a day. (*Pause*) I journeyed to Mexico City and got a plane to Los Angeles. (*He chuckles*) To get extra money for my dream of a trip, I got a job at Universal Studios, as a designer, and I worked on three films (*laughing and emphasising*) Three bad films. I quit after six months and continued my journey, LA to San Francisco.

The lights come on and the backdrop shows (repeatedly) Edmund's World trip drawings.

THE GHOST OF OLD EDMUND KARA: Then I boarded a cargo ship to the Philippines. I spent twenty one days at sea. The ship then headed for Hong Kong. (*He laughs*) Bizarrely, I was invited to a banquet in my honour by the Boys' Bicycle Club of South China! (*Pause*) Then it was on to Singapore and then a boat to British-occupied Ceylon. I hung around there for a month or so. (*Pause*)

He turns to the backdrop and turns back to the audience. He steps forward, to be more intimate.

I was sketching all the time, a visual diary of my experiences, to send to my mother and my siblings. Then a long ferryboat ride got me to India, to Bombay, heaving with humans like an unorganised army of ants, a city boisterous in its very being, and, God, the appalling poetry of its poverty. (*Pause*)

I took an English liner, which was on its way from Australia, to London. Then I headed for Marseilles. I met up with a cycling friend, Christine Brown, who had worked as a child physiotherapist in Canada, and we took in the whole of the Riviera and cycled over into Northern Italy. (*Pause*) I was ready to go back to America, and I returned to New York by boat. (*He laughs*) A couple of years of my life had rode away!

All darkens. **THE GHOST OF OLD EDMUND KARA** *exits the stage. Then we hear the start of Judy Garland singing 'Somewhere*

Over the Rainbow'. Then busy Hollywood-like music. Coloured swathes of light wash the stage quickly. The music gets louder. A photo of Hollywood fills the backdrop.

VOICE OF POET 1 (*shouting like a film director*): Hollywood! Hollywood! Hollywood! Hollywood!

The coloured swathes of light stop and the music goes down in volume. We see a lit-up white backdrop. Behind the backdrop, we see the silhouette of **YOUNG EDMUND KARA** *working at a desk, drawing. As* **THE GHOST OF OLD EDMUND KARA** *comes on to the right of the stage, the music goes up in volume.*

THE GHOST OF OLD EDMUND KARA (*loudly*): Los Angeles beckoned again, the pull of designing again and freelance work. I worked in a clothing shop in Beverly Hills, for a woman who had made clothes for Lena Horne. I got very settled into LA life. I had a charming little cottage in an avocado orchard. I did work for a film from Paramount Studios, one of the famous factories of fantasy, one of the makers of the mind's unreality. (*Pause*)

He glances at **YOUNG EDMUND KARA** *and then faces the audience.*

I worked and worked, designing for two labels, Jewel and Athena.

The two fashion models strut on to the stage, gaggling like geese (talking nonsense) and strut around **THE GHOST OF OLD EDMUND KARA**.

VOICE OF POET 1: (*like a film director*): Let's make money! Let's make money!

The loud sound of a money till.

VOICE OF POET 2: Let's make money! Let's make money!

The loud sound of a money till.

The two female fashion models strut more quickly and gaggle more noisily around **THE GHOST OF OLD EDMUND KARA**.

VOICES OF POETS 1 and 2 (*together*): Let's make money! Let's make money!

The loud sound of a money till.

VOICES OF POETS 1 and 2 (*hysterically*): Let's make money! Let's make money!

The loud sound of money till repeated in a manic way, louder and louder.

VOICES OF POETS 1 and 2 *(even more hysterically):* Let's make money! Let's make money!

The start of Judy Garland singing 'Somewhere Over the Rainbow' (repeated like a CD song that is faulty). The silhouette of **YOUNG EDMUND KARA** *stands up and cries desperately:* Stop! Stop! Stop! Stop! For Christ's sake, stop!

Judy Garland stops singing. The Hollywood-like music stops. The two female fashion models run off the stage, screaming in a silly way. The backdrop darkens until the silhouette of **YOUNG EDMUND KARA** *is not visible.* **THE GHOST OF OLD EDMUND KARA** *is spotlighted. He looks all around, bemused. The sound of a shrieking bird is heard. The spotlight shrinks to light just his face.* **THE BIRD DANCER**, *spotlighted, struts on to the stage and moves around* **THE GHOST OF OLD EDMUND KARA**, *slowly and curiously, then exits.*

THE GHOST OF OLD EDMUND KARA: I remember thinking, this is (*weight on the word*) <u>dead</u>. This is not the way I want to live the rest of my life. (*Pause*) 1962. (*Pause*) The song of myself began, ringing in my head like a bell of warning. Leave! Leave! Leave! Leave! That trip around the world was not just an outward journey. For me, it was an inward journey. I was going toward myself, toward the funeral pyre of the bad selves, which I needed to go up in wild feathers of flames. (*Pause*)

I was in the cul-de-sac of my life. I turned around and looked down a dusty road of possible truths. There was a sense of (*emphasising*) death on my tongue. I had to get away from the shining and false myths of LA. I was thirty-eight years old. (*Pause*) I quit the fashion industry, West Hollywood, and I moved to Big Sur.

The loud sounds of the ocean and the wind grow and grow in volume.

Curtain

Scene 2

The beating sound of American Native Indian drums begins. The backdrop behind **THE GHOST OF OLD EDMUND KARA**, *who is standing to the right of the backdrop, is showing Carolyn Mary Kleefeld's paintings of Edmund's cabin, repeatedly. The sound of the drums gets louder. Swathes of red light start to wash the stage.* **THE BIRD DANCER** *enters on to the stage, strutting. Then he starts to dance dramatically and frantically, using up all of the available stage space for several minutes (or longer). He and the drums suddenly stop. He stands, wings upright, for several moments in the silence. Then we hear the very loud sounds of a chisel carving into wood, repeatedly. Then some very loud hammering and some very loud sawing. Then silence.* **THE BIRD DANCER** *exits, strutting. The backdrop starts to show film and photos of Big Sur.* **THE GHOST OF OLD EDMUND KARA** *is spotlighted.*

THE GHOST OF OLD EDMUND KARA (*rhythmically*):

Here, the clutter
Of nonsense,
The politics
Of survival
Went out of my mind.

Here, it was the poetry
Of nature
That soothed my thoughts.

Here, the mischievous
Blow of the wind
Smoked the dust paths.

Here, the angels
Of sunlight
Teased the tall redwoods
Gathered like gods.

Here, the aloneness
Was crowded with silence.

The loud sound of the ocean and the wind.

THE GHOST OF OLD EDMUND KARA *(loudly):* I was trying to get away from that whole commercial world. I stopped thinking about being a successful artist. I just wanted to do it, and have *(emphasising)* <u>pure</u> creative freedom.

The sound of the ocean and the wind go down in volume.

VOICES OF POETS 1 and 2 (*together and rhythmically*):

He stood
Evening time,
Letting
The rhythms,
The masterful rhyme,
The moving prayer,
The telling
Swell
Of the ocean
Calm
The depths
Of his mind.

He stood,
Hearing
As clear as truth,
The music

Of a memory
Mislaid
By
Birth.

THE GHOST OF OLD EDMUND KARA (*fondly*):

In this suburb of Atlantis, (*he laughs*) beauty dripped in each moment. My life became pregnant with the humbling and sacred energy of this paradise at the edge of the world. (*Pause*) I began to connect with the cosmic forces, the sensual fruits of life, the eternity-glazed furniture of nature, the mind's illuminations of focused observing. I began to see how the extraordinary resides in the ordinary, how there are deep wells in the surfaces of things. How the landscape is a work of art, confirming the creator, the life-force, in its silent retreats and the holiness of its many symphonies of songs.

VOICE OF POET 1 (*rhythmically*):

The orchestra
Of insects
Unseen
Performing
On the ocean's
Edge.

A flare of protests,
An urgent humming,
Loud tiny music,
Up against *(pause)*
The wash of the waves.

THE GHOST OF OLD EDMUND KARA (*fondly*): The whole of my being was open to all that surrounded me. My bohemian senses were tuned into the ever-present process of life.

The backdrop shows a photo of a giant cactus.

VOICE OF POET 2 *(rhythmically)*:

Giant Cactus: Big Sur *(pause)*

A cluster of green blades,
A slow growth of sculptured stillness

Taller than a man.
A Buddha of a plant.

A threatening stance
And flames of praise.

THE GHOST OF OLD EDMUND KARA: And death.

The backdrop shows a photo of a dead cactus.

VOICE OF POET 1 *(rhythmically)*:

Dead Giant Cactus: Big Sur *(pause)*

Corpse of an alien,
Ash-grey.

Pathetic limbs
Of impotent leaves.

Spidery bone
Of a body.

A dried-out
Piece of beach wood.

A sculpture
Of skeletal fingers.

No longer pepper-green, (*pause*)
No longer flaring.

The backdrop shows photos of Big Sur.

THE GHOST OF OLD EDMUND KARA: Ah, life *(emphasising)* and death. (*Pause*) The ever-teasing mysteries for humankind. The birth of a wave, the death of a wave. The mischievous sweet birds fluttering from bush to bush, with their living code of poems, and the clinical machine of the searching hawk, its arrogant glide and its fabulous eyes of death. (*Pause*) I liked looking at life straight in the face. I liked seeing it for what it really is and stripping it of any cosmetic doctoring or glamorising. (*Pause*) Here I became very aware of the power that is infused in all of life from every star in the heavens to every minnow in the sea. I began to believe in a central seed consciousness that is fused in all of the universe. The visual manifestation of it for all humans is in their Earth-bound existence, in all that is seen and felt. (*Pause*) Many, many times, I stood or sat on the balcony of this cabin and I watched a full moon on its stage of the starry sky, my mind mesmerised and my soul aching with its raw detachment.

The backdrop shows a photo of a full moon over Big Sur. Then a photo of the moon fills the backdrop.

VOICE OF POET 1 (*slowly, rhythmically, and with confidence*):

Full Moon, Big Sur (*pause*)

I light up
The white flowers,
Torches
That now worship the seeds in my sky.

I dazzle the limp pool
Where the Eve-shaped woman,

As pale as my smile,
Swims in my dream.

I polish
The trunks of the trees
With their growing thoughts
Of my silver blood.

I manifest
My eternity
In the goddess eyes
Of a statued cat.

I startle
The strange, gripped land
With my tiring milk
Of coldness.

I claim
The night's far borders
With the diamond thirst
Of my depths.

I drug
The renegade moments
With the ancient spell
Of my silence.

And I make
The metallic muscles
Of the ocean,
Flexing their flow of energy,

Carry the cargoes
Of my tambourine soul.

The backdrop shows film or photos of the Pacific Ocean.

THE GHOST OF OLD EDMUND KARA:

The metallic muscles
Of the ocean,
Flexing their flow of energy.

(*Pause*)

There's a giant sexual energy in the sculptures I made. A primal energy. I always had an ocean of sexual energy in me. My move to Big Sur was a desire to pour it into my creative work. To utilise the drama of the masculine and feminine energies in me.

He turns to look at the backdrop.

And my cliff-edge cabin, my home and my studio, designed and built by me, rang day and night, night and day, with the constant deep mantra of the ocean's energy. It was the dominant musical score to my life, my work, and my leisure. Its mountain of music avalanched into my sleep and rolled over in my castaway dreams. It was the god-like, goddess-like, companion to my every moment.

The spotlight on **THE GHOST OF OLD EDMUND KARA** *goes out. The stage is in darkness but for the backdrop. The loud sound of the ocean for several moments. Then it goes down in volume.*

VOICES OF POETS 1 and 2 (*in harmony, powerfully, and their voices recorded to sound like 4 to 6 voices speaking like a choral group*):

The sea insists
On an old rag of a song,
As a lone boat
Is bashed by a bay of a wind.

The sea persists with its
Kettledrum throng, a waterfall
Gong calling a storm.

Bones, bedded
In the cellar of time,
Moan and groan;
Their surfaced cries
Thrash the walls of the world.

The sighs of fathers
And sons rise
From below
To bellow and blow
In the loveless night.

Waves argue over rocks
And knock on the doors
Of the clouds.

Each breath of the sea
Is heavier
Than a whale;
Each movement of its force
Is sleeker than a shark.

Water praising the boom of its phrases;
Water banging
El Sur grande;
Haranguing time
With its life and its death.

A commotion
Of emotion; a rhythm
Unfolding;
Battle chants battering
The Earth's sleeping face.

It is the sea of Big Sur,
Shadowed by the soul

Of the moon,
Erasing the flesh
Of the land.

It is not even a moment
In the mood
Of the mind of creation,
This ocean washing
The bowl of a dream.

The backdrop darkens. The face of **THE GHOST OF OLD EDMUND KARA** *is spotlighted.*

THE GHOST OF OLD EDMUND KARA: So death was no longer on my tongue only an insatiable thirst for life. My solitary life here in Big Sur. I knew that I wanted to sculpt, and that's what I was going to do here. I wanted the physical challenge of working (*emphasising*) dead wood into (*emphasising*) living art. (*Pause*)

I had trained in art school and I had so enjoyed doing some beach carvings in LA one summer. Out of the ashes of the costume designer would come the fire of a sculptor! I would start with a phoenix bird, in honour of my rebirth!

The spotlight dims and goes out, until the stage is in darkness. **THE GHOST OF OLD EDMUND KARA** *exits the stage. The loud sound of chiselling, hammering, and sawing. The white backdrop is lit-up. Behind the backdrop, we see the silhouette of* **YOUNG EDMUND KARA***, who is chiselling, hammering, and sawing at a stump of wood, which is taller than him.* **THE GHOST OF OLD EDMUND KARA** *comes on to the right of the stage. The sounds of* **YOUNG EDMUND KARA** *working go down in volume.*

THE GHOST OF OLD EDMUND KARA: I was a very dear friend of Lolly Fassett, who was building the Phoenix Shop at the bottom of Nepenthe Restaurant on Big Sur's Highway 1. In fact, I was her tenant when I first arrived in Big Sur. (*Pause*) Nepenthe, in its time, attracted those lit-up by success and fame, such as Clint Eastwood, Steve McQueen, Joan Baez, and, of course, Elizabeth Taylor and Richard Burton. (*Pause*) It also attracted those lit-up by non-success and non-fame, such as beatniks, bohemians, and hippies. (*He laughs*) Ah, I (*emphasising*) did love Nepenthe. Really loved it. Anyway, Lolly and I got around to talking about the Phoenix bird and its resurrection symbolism. (*Pause*) The terrace of Nepenthe had once boasted a beautiful, elderly oak tree. It was the first thing people saw when they climbed the ramp through the gardens. Thanks to some bad gardening, the much-loved oak tree went to its unexpected death. (*Pause*)

I looked out of the window of my rented lodgings one day, and down in Mule Canyon I saw this giant hunk of redwood that had fallen down into the creek. So I called a guy named Hugh Fleenor, who knew how to use heavy machinery. He came down and hauled it out.

He turns to look at the silhouetted **YOUNG EDMUND KARA**, *working away at the stump of wood, and then faces the audience again.*

THE GHOST OF OLD EDMUND KARA (*proudly*): I would work up to fourteen hours a day and night, if necessary.

The white backdrop darkens.

THE GHOST OF OLD EDMUND KARA: I sculpted it in one piece and made its legs and claws of bronze. It weighed as heavy as a Greek god!

The white backdrop is lit-up. We see the silhouetted **YOUNG EDMUND KARA** *standing alongside a silhouette of* **THE BIRD DANCER**, *standing sideways with his wings up.*

THE GHOST OF OLD EDMUND KARA: In 1976, my Phoenix Bird clawed its bronze feet into the upright stump of that ancient oak tree on the terrace of Nepenthe. (*He laughs*) Aloe Vera was planted around the oak tree stump, to become the green flames of nature.

VOICE OF POET 2 *(slowly and rhythmically):*

Aloe Vera:
Green flames
Licking
The pagan mind;

Wild tongues
Voicing
A hymn
To a bird;

Fingers almost
Touching
A myth's
Golden words;

Nests of fire;
Crab-like fronds
Of verdant
Passion;

Green flames
Worshipping
A sculptor's
Slow dream.

THE GHOST OF OLD EDMUND KARA: A wooden bench for visitors surrounded all.

He looks at the lit-up white backdrop.

THE GHOST OF OLD EDMUND KARA: *(exclaiming)* The phoenix had risen!

Curtain

ACT TWO

Scene 1

The sound of lively, violin-fiddling music. The backdrop shows a photo of Edmund Kara's Phoenix Bird at Nepenthe. Six people, wearing elaborate Halloween masks and costumes, are seated at tables, chatting away. Bottles of wine and glasses are on the tables. A sign on a post states: NEPENTHE'S BAL MASQUE/FUNDRAISING FOR THE BIG SUR FIRE BRIGADE. *The music gets more boisterous. Red and green lights start to swathe quickly across the stage, as photos of Edmund Kara's sculptured masks fill the backdrop, though we see the photo of the Phoenix Bird intermittently.* **YOUNG EDMUND KARA**, *wearing one of his redwood masks (a cardboard copy of a photo of one will do) and a long Halloween gown, enters the stage on the right. There is a theatrical confidence to his entrance. The seated people turn to watch his entrance and clap enthusiastically as he moves to centre stage.*

YOUNG EDMUND KARA (*loudly above the music, which goes down in volume*): My (*emphasising*) <u>favourite</u> holiday is Halloween, the artist's holiday. A chance to lose your identity and feel what's in the mask. It's a chance to be (*he laughs*) a chameleon. (*Pause*) I had a facial fixation as a boy and loved to study the anatomical structure of different faces. I (*emphasising*) love to carve faces, it's an endlessly interesting challenge to achieve the transition of forms.

The backdrop changes to a photo of the large, outdoor fireplace (the fire is alight) at Nepenthe. The seated people stand and start to dance in a flamboyant way around **YOUNG EDMUND KARA**. *Then the dancers start to strut (like the female fashion models earlier in Act One) and gaggle like geese at the back of* **YOUNG EDMUND KARA**, *using the full length of the stage. As the music stops, the people stop strutting and line up behind* **YOUNG EDMUND KARA**. *All darkens. There is the incessant sound of the wind. It gets louder and louder. Then, at first, the slow heartbeat rhythm of American Native Indian drums, which get faster and faster. The wind competes with the drums. The sound of the wind stops. The eerie screech of a bird. The slow heartbeat rhythm of American Native Indian drums. Silence. Red light fills the stage, which is still the Nepenthe Bal Masque scene/staging.* **YOUNG EDMUND KARA**, *still in his mask and costume, is centre stage. The Nepenthe people are standing, perfectly still, either side of him, still in their masks and costumes. Their hands are behind their backs. The backdrop shows a photo of Edmund's 'Sleeping Diana' sculpture. In front of the backdrop, on the stage, there is a heap of dark blankets.*

YOUNG EDMUND KARA (*emotionally but in control*): My beloved sister, Diana, whom we called Dinka, had a beautiful face. I have always had a concern for beauty, form, line, and proportions. (*Pause for several moments*) She hanged herself before my move to Big Sur. My fellow fashion labourer in New York. (*Pause*) My baby sister. (*Pause*) My princess of her sewing machine (*Pause*) Her beautiful (*emphasising*) <u>mask</u> of a face. How can the human mind, the human heart, the human soul ever blow away the dust of dark grief?

The Nepenthe people reveal a hangman's noose in their hands. **YOUNG EDMUND KARA** *takes a chisel and hammer from under his gown. The sound of chiselling and hammering starts. One by one,* **YOUNG EDMUND KARA** *mimics chiselling and hammering away at each person. As he does so, each person goes into a sculpture-like pose (one kneeling, one hands in the air, one arms across the chest etc., whatever looks dramatic). He grabs a dark blanket and, one by one, fully covers each person.* **YOUNG EDMUND KARA** *turns to the audience and he holds up his chisel and hammer to the heart area of his body.*

<u>Curtain</u>

Scene 2

The backdrop shows some photos of Edmund's cabin before its dereliction. In front of the backdrop is a large bench and a stool. A stump of wood is on the bench, plus chisels, a hammer, a saw, paint brushes, and rags. The loud sounds of the ocean and the wind. The backdrop changes to photos of Edmund's various sculptures and stops on a photo of Edmund's studio wall and some of his hung sculptures. **YOUNG EDMUND KARA** *enters. He has a lit cigarette in one hand. He sits on the stool, facing the audience. The sounds of the ocean go down in volume but still contribute to the atmosphere.*

YOUNG EDMUND KARA *(puffing occasionally on his cigarette):*

Each morning, I come in to my cave of a workshop, the cramped cellar of my wooden cabin, which is damp with the ocean's wide cloud of a fog.

Each morning, like a blacksmith in a forge, at his anvil, I labour with my chosen wood.

As my thoughts go into the core of the wood, pale autumn leaves fall to the floor.

Each morning, under the white spray of one spotlight, until dawn breaks as brash as a rooster, I chisel away at the stump that is hiding a vision.

Each morning, I *(emphasising the words)* <u>chip</u> and <u>shape</u>, <u>hit</u> and <u>strike</u>, work to the music of my slow craft's tools.

As my thoughts go into the core of the wood, pale autumn leaves fall to the floor.

Each morning, my bench is the operating table for a surgeon of wood.

Each morning, the Pacific Ocean busies itself below, carves its centuries of ebb and flow into the land, and smoothes the breasts of its claim of rocks.

As my thoughts go into the core of the wood, pale autumn leaves fall to the floor.

Some mornings, the sunlight butters the windows and flames the colours of my stained-glass window.

Some mornings the eerie shroud of the fog smothers the view with its coldness and strangeness.

As my thoughts go into the core of the wood, pale autumn leaves fall to the floor.

Each morning, the wood reveals a problem, a stubbornness not to become other than it is.

Each morning, my struggle becomes more clear as I get more near the dream in my mind.

As my thoughts go into the core of the wood, pale autumn leaves fall to the floor.

He stubs out his cigarette and re-lights another one from a packet in his pocket. He stands up and moves closer to the audience.

YOUNG EDMUND KARA *(occasionally puffing on his cigarette):* I'm a worker. I belong to the working-class. I love physical labour, that's why I chose wood. Painting and drawing were too contemplative for me, and I didn't use this driving, forceful energy I have. I have this outrageous energy and very good discipline. I get caught up in whatever I am making. I work very hard when I do my sculpting, ten to twelve hours a day. And I work on one sculpture at a time. I like craft, I've always liked craft. I can paint, draw, sew. (*Proudly*) I can build a house. It's all pleasure to me.

The backdrop starts to show photos of redwoods in a forest, stumps etc.

YOUNG EDMUND KARA (*slowly moving about the stage*): I'm in love with trees, especially redwoods. Those giants that gather in a silent conspiracy. Those giants that stretch their strong trunks up, and up, and up, to praise the moon, to praise the sun. Those giants that stand sturdy as totem poles and demand a kind of worship themselves. (*Pause*)

I'm interested in their abandoned stumps, weather-broken, man-dumped, slumped in a canyon; a lump of wood in a shade of earth as dark as an evening cemetery; a tree's corpse laid to rest by a busy stream, which is dreaming its way through the gentle grass. (*Pause*)

Stumps that are imprisoning shapes which long to be freed by the tools of my trade. Stumps that will obsess me like a brand-new lover, which will possess my time, my mind, my heart and my soul. (*Pause*)

Stumps that will strait-jacket my thoughts, present me with physical problems. Stumps where my labouring will sing with the grain. Stumps with the possibilities of rhythms, the hidden poem in the history of a forest. (*Pause*)

Stumps with an innate prayer only I can hear. Stumps with the deep sob of humanity's grief. Stumps that are like coffins holding prophets or peasants within. Stumps where the seven deadly sins reside with their temptations. (*Pause*)

Stumps where a bird nests inside, waiting to rise with its wings like flames. (*Pause*)

I am interested in wood, redwood, where ideas sleep until I awaken them. (*Longer pause*)

I'm in love with the thought of (pause and then emphasising passionately) the fire in the wood.

He sits back on the stool. The backdrop shows Edmund's studio wall again.

YOUNG EDMUND KARA: I work with pieces of wood that have come to me, gifts from friends, neighbours, from the beach below. I have used snarls of madrone, chunks of cherry, big knots of oak, and *(he laughs)* stumps of redwood. (*Pause*) I have a passive attitude about my own creations. I don't want to go and find the wood. I like the challenge of making art out of what life has presented as an art problem. I never have an idea first that I try to find the wood for. I invent my sculptures as I go along. (*He laughs*) Though this recluse living on a suburb of Atlantis has done some large sculpted doors (*laughs again*), commissions I suppose, for the likes of Clint Eastwood and the Congregation Beth Israel in Carmel Valley. (*Pause*) But my sculptures have nothing to do with money or what somebody wants, they have to do with myself. I don't have to satisfy any public taste or think commerce. (*He stands up and takes a few steps to the left and then to the right. He stands still. (Passionately*) Capitalism annihilates creativity because you start working for bucks, rather than just working to be an artist. (*Pause*) Other sculptors make their statement their way, and I can't accept any of their styles or fashion as a guide post for myself. (*Pause*) I used to go to see the museums in New York, the Museum of Modern Art etc., and I'd admire the sculptures that moved me. I have to examine my own feelings. (*Long pause*) The less distraction, the more intense the focus.

He sits, puffing at his cigarette.

VOICE OF POET 1 (*in a critic's authoritative voice*): Beginning with a piece of wood, Kara pares away unwanted protrusions with large saws, then reduces the wooden mass further with chisels and mallets, rasps, rifflers, and sandpaper. Work-time ranges from several weeks to many months.

VOICE Of POET 2 (*in a critic's authoritative voice*): Confronted with Kara's work, words such as (*emphasising each word*) <u>organic</u>, <u>figurative</u>, <u>metaphorical</u>, <u>movement</u>, <u>swirl</u>, <u>elemental</u>, <u>meticulous</u>, <u>abstract</u>, <u>fluid</u>, <u>flowing</u>, <u>sensuous</u>, <u>energy</u>, <u>erotic</u>, <u>evocative</u>, <u>mythical</u>, <u>magical</u>, <u>dramatic</u>, <u>primordial</u>, <u>pagan</u>, and <u>poetic</u> enters the minds of those privileged to enter his studio in his cabin.

YOUNG EDMUND KARA *stands up and picks up a chisel and hammer.*

YOUNG EDMUND KARA *(proudly, almost boastful):* My love of wood is a genetic gift from an old line of wood-workers and cabinet makers in Russia. (*Emphasising*) <u>Wood</u> is my tongue.

<u>**Curtain**</u>

Scene 3

The opening section of the song 'The Shadow of your smile'. The backdrop shows photos of Big Sur (such as Bixby Bridge, Pfeiffer Beach) and stops on a photo of Elizabeth Taylor and Richard Burton on Pfeiffer Beach. To the right of the stage, **YOUNG EDMUND KARA** *is standing by a stump of wood taller than him. His hair is pulled back into a ponytail. He is wearing flip-flop sandals and he is holding a chisel and a hammer. The loud sound of the ocean and the wind. He mimics chipping away at the stump of wood.*

VOICE OF POET 2 (*like a news reporter*): 1965. THE SANDPIPER film is in full production, starring A-list Hollywood stars Elizabeth Taylor, Richard Burton, and Eva Marie Saint and Charles Bronson. Directed by Vincent Minnelli, based on a story written by producer Martin Ransohoff, with music by Johnny Mandel. It is an MGM production. (*Pause*) Being filmed on location in beautiful, rugged Big Sur. (*Pause*)

Taylor is playing Laura Reynolds, an unmarried single mother and artist, mother to Danny. They live in a secluded cabin on the edge of the sea of Big Sur. Circumstances and Californian law lead her to Doctor Reverend Edward Hewitt, being played by Burton, who is headmaster at an Episcopal Boarding School and married to teacher Claire, being played by Eva Marie Saint. (*Pause*) Despite their religious differences, amplified by Laura's atheistic dislike of religion, Edward begins a passionate extra-marital affair. (*Pause*) The affair comes to light and Edward and Claire agree to a trial separation. Edward resigns as headmaster and plans to do some travelling. (*Pause*) The sandpiper bird, with its broken wing, which is healed by Laura to regain its freedom, is the film's main motif of personal development and freedom.

YOUNG EDMUND KARA *stops chiseling and turns to face the audience. He lights up a cigarette.*

YOUNG EDMUND KARA (*occasionally puffing on his cigarette*): I purposefully leave each area to develop as I'm going. I work occasionally around the piece. At a certain moment, all of a sudden, the light flashes on what I'll do with this area, and I'll may be rough it in then, and then move on for awhile, until some gestation period goes by and some puzzles get solved. And then I'll come back to it. (*Pause*) You're faced with a chaotic mass that you would like to re-organise merely using your substance as clay. It's like an unveiling. Sometimes I see it in an instant, sometimes later. You're taking a risk, a chance, a decision, all that excitement is there every moment of it. (*Pause, then dramatically*) It is getting pregnant. (*Pause*) It is creation. (*Pause*) It is birth.

All darkens for several moments. Then there is just a spotlight on the face of **YOUNG EDMUND KARA**.

YOUNG EDMUND KARA (*slowly and rhythmically*):

Today,
A clouded walk,
A clouded mind.

Last night,
The gremlins
Of insomnia
Dishevelled
My sleep.

I woke
To the tiredness
Of an old man;

A shroud of thick fog
Thrown over my soul.

As I stepped out,
I took bits
Of my hell
Into paradise.

VOICE OF POET 1 (*like a news reporter*): The scene Saturday along the spectacular road below Carmel looked like a movie of a movie being made. At Bill Fassett's Nepenthe, a camera crew was shooting a group of folk dancers for a trailer that will precede THE SANDPIPER and explain Big Sur to the world. (*Pause*) In a nearby studio a shaggy and talented wood sculptor named Edmund Kara was putting the finishing touches on a nude redwood torso of Miss Taylor, an object that plays an important role in the film. (*Pause*) 'For one thing,' said Edmund, 'it gets some nudity into the picture.' He gazed lovingly at her 38" bust. 'I didn't have to measure her,' he said. 'I used to be a dress designer, I just (emphasizing) know.'

The spotlight goes out and the lights come on. The backdrop shows another photo of Elizabeth Taylor and Richard Burton from THE SANDPIPER film. **YOUNG EDMUND KARA** *is by the stump of wood, chisel and hammer in his hands, and facing the audience.*

YOUNG EDMUND KARA: I consider the very essence of my work to be about hair. Trees are the hairs of the earth. I like to express hair, in my work as what I call supra-cilia. It's about the organic flow. It's the link in my work.

He puts his chisel and hammer on the stool. He goes off stage and returns with a large white blanket. He places it over the stump of wood, covering it completely. He stands still, looking at the backdrop. The backdrop shows film of Edmund working on the Elizabeth Taylor sculpture. We hear the loud sound of the ocean and wind intermingled with an excerpt from 'The Shadow of Your Smile'. Sounds and music stop.

VOICE OF POET 2 (*like a news reporter*): Flash from Hollywood. (*Pause*) Liz Burton, as she likes to be called, has been many, many things in her lifetime. Last year, a painting of her and the late Marilyn Monroe was featured at New York's Whitney Museum Annual. (*Pause*) The painting was a fine work, but it didn't cause much of a stir. (*Pause*) But now there is a wood sculpt of her, rising naked from a tree stump, bird on shoulder. Edmund Kara's twenty-five thousand dollar statue of the modern goddess is being used to promote THE SANDPIPER, which certainly explains the bird on her shoulder.

VOICE OF POET 1 (*like a news reporter*): A naked Ms. Taylor never sat for Big Sur sculptor Edmund Kara, but a life-cast plaster mask was provided. In fact, a dear friend of Kara's, jazz singer Stella Brooks, with whom Kara said shared a similar body type to the A-list actress, posed. We are sure Welshman Richard Burton was more than happy with the arrangement.

The backdrop shows film of Richard Burton and Edmund Kara in Paris for the unveiling.

VOICE OF POET 1 (*like a news reporter*): The finished nude sculpture of Hollywood star Elizabeth Taylor, by Big Sur-based Edmund Kara, which will feature in THE SANDPIPER film, was recently shipped to Paris aboard the Queen Mary. (*Pause*) The writer and producer of the film, Martin Ransohoff, hired a detective guard to accompany it. Though he booked a first-class room on board for the special creation, the statue ended up in the cargo hold because of shipping rules. The nude sculpture weighs in at 712 pounds and cargo is forbidden in first-class accommodations. The life-size nude statue was unveiled with much fanfare in a Paris art gallery by Richard Burton. Its creator Edmund Kara was present.

YOUNG EDMUND KARA (*mischievously*): And so I danced with the rich and famous again (*Pause*) but just for a while!

Curtain

ACT THREE

Scene 1

A replica (or back-drop photo or film) of Edmund's derelict cabin. The loud sound of the ocean and the wind. **THE GHOST OF OLD EDMUND KARA** *comes on to the stage, slowly, until he is centre stage. All darkens until only his face is spotlighted.*

THE GHOST OF OLD EDMUND KARA *(rhythmically and with cynicism):*

Fame is a false home. It is always ripe for demolition by the machines of jealousy.

Its rooms of success hide a deep emptiness. Its doors are open to the marble-eyed wolves that wait around like sheep.

Fame is a place of madness, an asylum for four-faced egos.

Fame is a terrible place.

It is a residence on rotten stilts. It has spaces where the soul is bartered out and where the self dies in a circle of mirrors.

Fame is a house where a blessing is married to a curse.

Fame has windows that are the eyes of enemies, a swimming pool that drowns reality.

Fame is a shaky property that sits on a lonely hill.

Fame is a stranger out in the world, using your name and living parts of your life.

Fame is a terrible place.

He is silent for several moments.

THE GHOST OF OLD EDMUND KARA: Did I hope, want, plan to shape fame and success out of wood? (*Emphasising*) <u>No</u>, I was chiseling, hammering, sawing out paths towards some kind of truth. (*Pause*) In my weather-blitzed womb of a home, this workshop that gave birth to my theatre of characters, I tried to carve out my dreams and visions. I laboured into the hours, trying to get to the (*emphasizing*) <u>core</u> of my dreams and visions, to the fire in the wood—and always, always failing.

The sound of chiseling, hammering, and sawing begins to intermingle with the sound of the ocean and the wind. All darkens. When the lights come on, **YOUNG EDMUND KARA** *is behind the lit-up backdrop. He is standing by a stump of wood, chiseling and hammering away at it.* **THE GHOST OF OLD EDMUND KARA** *moves to the right of the stage and faces the audience.*

THE GHOST OF OLD EDMUND KARA (*laughs*): After a dispute with a guy connected to THE SANDPIPER sculpture, I sawed it in half! I kept the head and sent the tits and torso to him! I attached a note (*emphasising*) CALL ME, and my cabin phone number!

He laughs for a few moments.

When I did saw the bloody thing in half, an army of mad termites poured out of it! Ah, (*pause*) the eager parasites of fame and success! So I went on my solitary search, a solitary person. My work was strictly self-discovery. I had had enough of the Sodom and Gomorrah of fame and success, and the ever-hungry ego for both fantasies. (*Pause*) I became like Garbo. I (*emphasising*) <u>wanted</u> to be alone (*he laughs*).

He turns to look at **YOUNG EDMUND KARA** *working. He faces the audience.*

THE GHOST OF OLD EDMUND KARA: I did have a poodle, named Guru, for fourteen years, a gift from a Big Sur lady. But, to tell the truth, I was always a very aloof person. I had relationships sexual, sensual, friends but any time they began to demand anything of me, or fit me into a picture with a frame around it, I stepped out of it. I was outta of there! *(He chuckles)* I didn't like anything to jeopardise my sense of freedom and liberty. Even as a boy, I never wanted to be in a team. I tended to like anything you could do by yourself, swimming, hiking, drawing, sculpting, and reading. *(Pause)* And I never joined any religious teams, including the Jewish religion of my family. I'm sure that was a disappointment for my beloved mother, Anna.

He turns to look at **YOUNG EDMUND KARA** *working. He faces the audience.*

THE GHOST OF OLD EDMUND KARA: Part of why I particularly loved sculpting in wood is because I didn't have to have conversations with people about material. I didn't have to buy anything. All I needed were my tools, which I did buy, and then I got lost in my studio. And the wood was just lying there, waiting in a forest somewhere, or there was a piece of wood leftover in a building site, or somebody would give me some bridge timber. *(Pause)*.

I liked everything around me in perfect order, and then I could work, just as long as I did not have any kind of disturbances. I couldn't have a dish in the sink or anything that was out of order. Everything had to look great. I liked visual beauty. And then I could work. *(Pause)*

I would listen to the birds in the trees with their worry of songs; the wind fondling my home, sometimes violently; and the ever-present, huge collapsing of the Pacific Ocean below my workshop. And the sounds of my breathless labouring tools would compete with the music of the natural forces. (*Pause and then laughs*)

I've had some very dramatic experiences with pieces, and with myself. I've had fights and arguments, and I've seen things fail that I had to make right. I have *(emphasising)* <u>burned</u> pieces that I felt were failures. I was never trying to get a message across in a sculpture, but there were messages nonetheless hidden ones and those felt by the handful who saw them. (*Pause*) I never wanted to make anything that I've seen before, or that's been made before, or that's become so hackneyed and cliched. If anything enters my mind that even smells of that, I don't want it because there's no adventure there. (*Pause*)

But, for me, it was the waiting for the mass, the wood, to manifest itself. That was where the adventure was and that was what inspired me. I was living an adventure, living a discovery of myself, and the possibilities of transferring the inner adventure into a reality. I didn't want to think about other artists. I wanted to discover what I could do. (*Pause*) I liked fairytales and myths. I liked classical subjects. I had a fantasy mind. I always wanted to do something that expressed an intense sense of beauty. (*Pause*)

Turning art into a business just didn't work for me. I did all that in New York and Hollywood when I was very young. Oh, I was once coaxed by my artist neighbour on the mountain above my cabin, to exhibit in her LA gallery. It was a retrospective exhibition in 1990. She was a dear, dear friend but it was a mere blip in my stubborn dislike of all the wine-drinking, cheese-nibbling nonsense of art's networking business. I sold one bloody piece!

He laughs and moves slowly about the stage.

THE GHOST OF OLD EDMUND KARA: And so I worked and worked at my family of sculptures for almost forty years. And in between I would go into Carmel or Monterey for groceries, driving my old turquoise car like a mad man. (*He laughs*) And I'd go and see good and (*emphasising*) <u>bad</u> films in the nearest cinema, meet friends in Nepenthe. (*Pause*) How I loved the Bal Masque there on Halloween night all those years ago! And I would have my handful of friends, such as Oscar, Glen, and my artist neighbour around to the cabin for (*he laughs*) our profound chats, for a meal. (*He laughs*) Usually greeting them with just a towel around my waist and my old radio mumbling away.

All darkens. The sounds of the ocean, the wind, the chiseling, hammering and sawing stop.

THE VOICE OF THE GHOST OF OLD EDMUND KARA: And then death was (*emphasising*) <u>really</u> on my tongue.

The sound of a shrieking bird is heard.

<u>Curtain</u>

Scene 2

The backdrop shows Carolyn Mary Kleefeld's paintings of Edmund Kara's cabin. They change quickly to create a really disturbing effect for a minute or more. Then all darkens. Spotlighted, the **ARTIST NEIGHBOUR ON THE MOUNTAIN** *enters on to the stage. She is carrying a handful of fresh flowers. She stands centre stage.*

ARTIST NEIGHBOUR ON THE MOUNTAIN: We sat with Edmundo in his candle-lit theater of a poetic lair which he had built thirty years before. His house was an extension of him, with its threadbare materials of deep burgundies and browns – deteriorating. (*Pause*)

A few weeks earlier, his doctor had announced: "You have a slow-growing bladder cancer and little can be done." Now, after his surgery, Edmundo stood like a tree bent over by the storms. He felt compelled to tell us about the horrid apparatus he had to endure for two weeks. My lover and I became overwhelmed by the force of his powerful energies. When he exclaimed, "I'm a control freak," I reminded myself to keep my own composure. (*Pause*)

Edmundo was so very authoritative and we so very not. The phone kept ringing, his friends wondering how he was. My lover and I went outside to his deck above the lyrical seas and I peered into his living room. In half profile, he seemed intensely focused even though engaged in just a casual phone conversation. He looked as if he was from another era, not to mention another realm. An underworld sea god, an archetypal power, he was both oppressive and inspiring in his gothic galleon of a home, with its Venetian flair, in commune with the wild seas below. (*Pause*)

I cried wildly "You are your most noble sculpture, using yourself as your own media." After this exclamation there was that lapse in time where brave souls meet, and collaborate without words, in silent understanding of each other. (*Pause*)

Rising above a prognosis of a terminal illness and the physical pain he was forced to endure, he was even more the enlightened muse. Others may have crumbled to this season, but Edmundo rose to the challenge, surpassing even himself. He was far more enthusiastic than I had ever known him to be, speaking of museum possibilities for his magnificent 'Moses' – possibly 'John, the Baptist' and 'The Seven Deadly Sins.' Just before we parted, he sang, from the decade of his Hollywood days, 'Accentuate the Positive' and 'Don't Mess with Mr. In-between'. (*Pause*)

Life is not only ironic and peculiar but also, in its tragedies, seems to dole out a balance of blessings, although they may not be recognized as such at the time. After a lifetime of cultivation within his most intelligent being, his Kara tree was now bearing the golden fruits of his halcyon season, which would last beyond earthly grasp. (*Pause*)

In this eleventh hour, the Moses of himself was reaching out to the world in a whole new way. It was perfect timing for this sculpture to be possibly accepted and exhibited by a museum in New York. After all, he had been born nearby in New Jersey, was Jewish, and the Moses of him was ready for liberation. Now that his time on earth was limited, recognition could no longer corrupt the sacred intention of his work. Now the dark gods were liberating him through disease. Intuitively he was preparing himself and his work for this upcoming cosmic insemination. (*Pause*)

Edmundo's indomitable spirit was illumined, inspiring all those who had the capacity to behold this evolving sculpture of a master, the cultivation of a world by an ingenious creator. (*Pause*)

She places the flowers on the floor at the centre of the stage and exits. All darkens.

THE VOICE OF THE GHOST OF OLD EDMUND KARA:
There were sleepless nights as pain, silent and precise, carved its way into my body. I lie, awake, my mind shaping my thoughts of eternity. Oh, and the landscape, sky, and ocean were taunting me.

The sound of the ocean and the wind. The backdrop shows the night sky and the ocean.

VOICE OF POET 2 (*slowly and rhythmically*):

Unfolding, unfolding
Night dream;
Its slow-rushing, slow-rushing
Moments
Fondle
Black rock and earth,
Tongue the pockets
Of caves.
Its coming, coming
Movements
Hold sky and land
In a spell,
Torment a hard stirring
Of stars,
Lick the moon with its breath,
As it spills
The love semen of aeons.

THE VOICE OF THE GHOST OF OLD EDMUND KARA:
There were desert days as death, silent and precise, began to sculpt my destiny. I lie, tired, my confused mind exhibiting a weird gallery of memories. Oh, and the landscape, sky, and ocean were taunting me. Oh, that ocean's song of life (*hesitates*) and death!

The sound of the ocean and the wind. The backdrop shows the day sky and the ocean.

VOICE OF POET 1 (*slowly and rhythmically*):

Unknotting the centuries,
Tiring out time's
Movement of questions.

A goddess or god
Taunting the un-answering
Moments.

An invader
Of the contemporary
Solid.

Rough lover
Of Genesis' sculpture.
Harsh rush

Employed by the sun.
Restless music
Harbouring man's torment.

A life-force
Offering an eternal language
We don't understand.

A memory of a womb (*pause*)
Lullabying
A mind.

All darkens. Silence. Spotlighted, **THE BIRD DANCER** *delicately struts on to the stage and moves towards the flowers, centre stage, in a curious way. He moves to the left of the stage. Spotlighted,* **YOUNG EDMUND KARA** *comes on to the stage, wearing his Nepenthe Bal Masque mask. He picks up the flowers and exits.*

THE BIRD DANCER *exits. All darkens.* **THE GHOST OF OLD EDMUND KARA**, *wearing different clothes to signify he is* **OLD EDMUND KARA** *rather than* **THE GHOST OF OLD EDMUND KARA,** *enters very slowly (like a dying man) and stands in the centre of the stage. The backdrop quickly shows photos of New York, Los Angeles, Big Sur, Nepenthe, Elizabeth Taylor and Richard Burton, Edmund Kara's sculptures, and the derelict cabin. The photos are shown again as the two female fashion models, wearing white doctor's gowns and white high-heels, strut silently and respectfully on to the stage, around* **OLD EDMUND KARA**, *and exit.*

VOICE OF POET 2 *(softly):* Edmund Kara had cancer. He entered a hospice in Monterey in May 2001.

The **ARTIST NEIGHBOUR ON THE MOUNTAIN** enters on to the stage.

The **ARTIST NEIGHBOUR ON THE MOUNTAIN** *(tenderly):*

Within the Robes of Friendship *(pause)*

When I visited you last night,
my dearest of friends,
your illness of thought
fed upon me like a virus,
like a demon of death
devouring my flowered gardens,
ravaging them with bitterness,
fading them with your weariness,
the despair of melancholy.
Yet I recognize your feelings
sometimes as my own.

In the robes of friendship
come both ill and joyous spirits;
it is all a part of intimacy shared.

The ARTIST NEIGHBOUR ON THE MOUNTAIN *exits.* **OLD EDMUND KARA** *exits very slowly. All darkens. We see* **OLD EDMUND KARA** *standing, silhouetted, behind the lit-up white backdrop.*

THE VOICE OF OLD EDMUND KARA *(remembering in an affectionate way):*

The unruly fence of trees beyond my cabin.

The gentle acorns strewn like old hand-grenades.

The slow, determined crunch of my footsteps on the long dirt path.

The lizards quick-shuffling to the haven of the hedges.

The little buzz machines of the insects busy in their green homes.

The flames of the ferns waving their friendly feathers.

The horizon smudged by a snowfall of clouds.

The fussy whirring of the humming birds.

The tall conspiracy of redwoods caught by the spotlights of sun.

The laboured flap of pelicans across the rhythmic unfolding of the waves.

The fringing froth of the waves' collapse on stretched-out sand along the coast.

The ferocious wind bullying the thoughts of the mind.

The late afternoon gold riding the wings of a gull. *(Pause)*

The petals of wood dropping to the floor *(said ten times as his voice fades out)*

(Then unexpectedly with anger) Burn them! Burn my creations! Burn the lot!

The loud sounds of the ocean and wind intermingle with the sounds of chiseling, hammering, and sawing. Then silence. The heartbeats of an American Native Indian drum. **THE BIRD DANCER,** *silhouetted, struts around* **OLD EDMUND KARA** *and then dances delicately around him. The drum stops.*

VOICES OF POETS 1 and 2 *(in chorus and rhythmically):*

This is the bird of grief
Attended by his ghosts;
His long black wing outstretched
Like a psalm of sorrow.

All the hurt of man
Is weeping from his eye,
All the war of loving
Is breaking in his night.

This is the room's last shadow,
The mother-feathered pain;
This is the touch of nursing souls
Before the flight of change.

This is the bird of grief
That shrieks inside the blood,
Whose silence is the sound of death,
Whose talons are for love.

THE BIRD DANCER *gently coaxes* **OLD EDMUND KARA** *to the floor. They are a silhouetted heap. Suddenly and dramatically,* **THE BIRD DANCER** *rises and spreads its wings in tender triumph.*

The loud sounds of the ocean and the wind. Then they go down in volume.

VOICES OF POETS 1 and 2 *(together):* Edmund Kara, sculptor, who always tried to find the fire in the wood, died on May 27th, 2001. He leaves to an unknowing world many sculptures, including *(read like a list):*

The Seven Deadly Sins
Diaspora
Christ lives, Aphrodite reigns
Epiphany
Ritual Orgasm
Yin Yang Variation
Four Seasons
Bitch Goddess
Arachne
Absorption
The Oracle
Moses
Sleeping Diana (*pause*)
Firebird

VOICE OF POET 1 *(in a critic's authoritative voice):* Beginning with a piece of wood, Kara pared away unwanted protusions with large saws, then reduced the wooden mass further with chisels and mallets, rasps, rifflers and sandpaper. Work time ranged from several weeks to many months.

VOICE OF POET 2 *(in a critic's authoritative voice):* Confronted with Kara's work, words such as organic, figurative, metaphorical, movement, swirl, elemental, meticulous, abstract, fluid, flowing, sensuous, energy, erotic, evocative, mythical, magical, dramatic, primordial, pagan, and poetic enter one's mind.

VOICE OF POET 1 *(rhythmically):*

Edmund Kara's Derelict Cabin, Big Sur

Time and again,
On my daily walks,
I'm drawn to your home,
Your workshop lodged
Just above the Pacific.

It's as if I'm called,
Pulled by the bare soul
Of your broken place,
A shrine of dark wood,
Quickly eroding
On the nerves of the weather,
In the slow mouth
Of time as it gnaws.

I walk down the path
Once worn by your shadow.
Today, as I approach
It looks even sadder;
As I enter one door
Another one whines
Through its old wound
To the heart-aching sea,
Which is crashing
Relentlessly
At this world where you worked.

Fragments of the windows
Litter the deck floor.
They're as sharp as the tools
You once used to shape
Truths into wood:
And wood into truths.

The fireplace, it seems,
Is waiting for the flames

To warm a dead room
With a sudden hearth's blaze.

You became a recluse,
Shunning art's game
And the ego's long thirst,
Like a castaway
On an island
Alone with his dream.

Outside, I pass
The stark KEEP OUT,
Which the dangerous
And determined
Elements ignore.

Fog starts to fill the stage. **THE GHOST OF OLD EDMUND KARA** *enters the stage on the left.* **YOUNG EDMUND KARA** *enters the stage on the right. The fog thickens.*

THE GHOST OF OLD EDMUND KARA: I was only ever craving one thing—that's reunion with the One.

YOUNG EDMUND KARA *(directly)*: Come on, old man, let us shake hands on *(emphasising)* <u>our</u> life.

They walk towards each other. The fog covers them (hides them) before they are able to shake hands.

VOICES OF POETS 1 and 2 *(in chorus):*

Fog
Is a slow
And steady
Ghost,
Leaving

Its breath
Of dawn
Over
An unseen
Paradise.

Fog
Veils the eyes
Of the cabin
With graveyard
Silence,
And smokes
The long
And
Blurred-stroked
Moments.

Fog
Is a slow
And heavy cloud,
An old man's
Quilt
Pulled over
The ocean.

Fog
Is a strange
And lovely death,
Whose cold shroud
Fades out (*slightly louder*)
One man's
Story.

The <u>very</u> loud sound of the ocean and the wind.

<u>Curtain</u>

PHOTOS AND DRAWINGS SUPPLEMENT
Photos by Peter Thabit Jones

Edmund Kara's derelict cabin
© 2017 Peter Thabit Jones

Edmund Kara's derelict cabin
© 2017 Peter Thabit Jones

Edmund Kara's derelict cabin
© 2017 Peter Thabit Jones

Part of Edmund Kara's work area in the derelict cabin
© 2017 Peter Thabit Jones

Edmund Kara's studio in the derelict cabin
© 2017 Peter Thabit Jones

Part of the living area inside the derelict cabin
© 2017 Peter Thabit Jones

The Phoenix sculpture on the patio of Nepenthe Restaurant, Big Sur
© 2017 Peter Thabit Jones

The Phoenix sculpture
© 2017 Peter Thabit Jones

The Phoenix sculpture
© 2017 Peter Thabit Jones

The Phoenix sculpture
© 2017 Peter Thabit Jones

DRAWINGS BY
CAROLYN MARY KLEEFELD

Casa de la Edmundo
© 2017 Carolyn Mary Kleefeld

Edmund's Cabin
© 2017 Carolyn Mary Kleefeld

Memories
© 2017 Carolyn Mary Kleefeld

Octopus Pier
© 2017 Carolyn Mary Kleefeld

Theater of Rocks
© 2017 Carolyn Mary Kleefeld

Neptune's Castle
© 2017 Carolyn Mary Kleefeld

Song of the Sea
© 2017 Carolyn Mary Kleefeld

Edmund Kara at work
© 2017 Walter Chappell

**Peter at the Edmund Kara Retrospective exhibition,
Sand City, California, July 2016**
© 2017 Peter Thabit Jones

Peter next to Miss Sur by Edmund Kara
© 2017 Patricia Holt

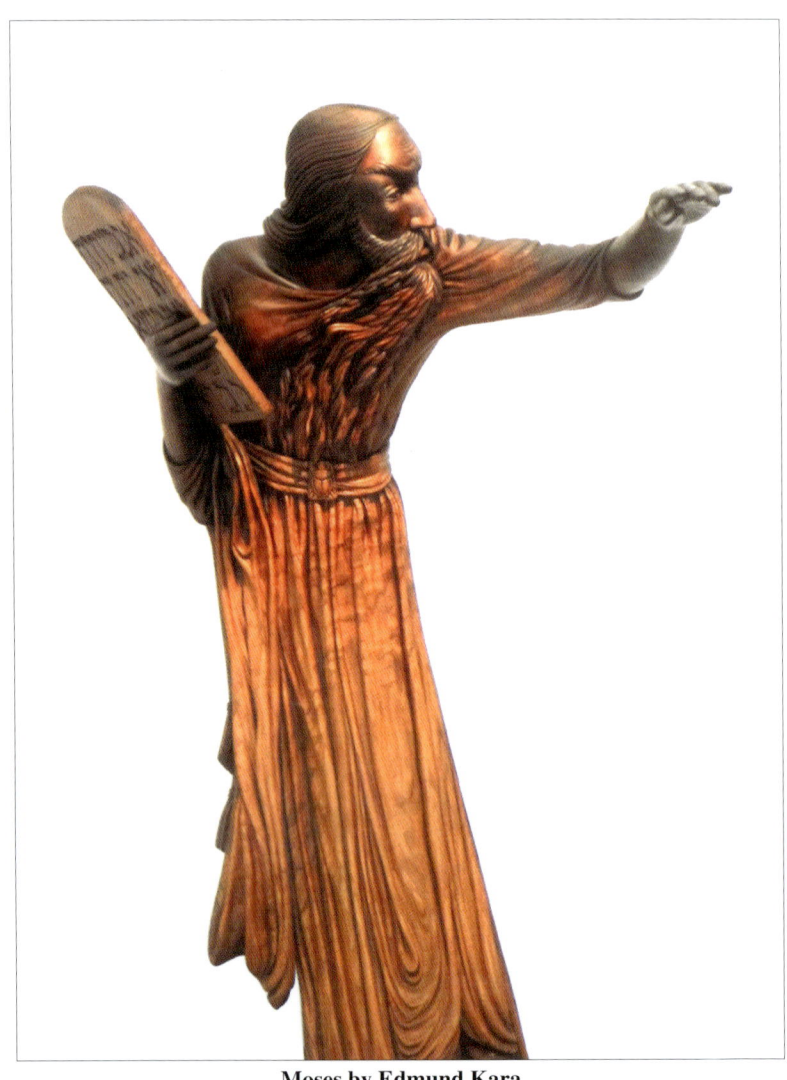

Moses by Edmund Kara
© 2017 Patricia Holt

Hidden in Hair by Edmund Kara
© 2017 Peter Thabit Jones

Part of The Seven Deadly Sins by Edmund Kara
© 2017 Peter Thabit Jones

Peter Thabit Jones inside Edmund Kara's studio
© 2017 Peter Thabit Jones

ABOUT THE AUTHOR

Peter Thabit Jones was born in Wales and raised by his maternal grandparents. He is the author of thirteen books, several of which have been reprinted and four published in Romania. His work has been translated into over twenty languages.

In March 2008 Peter's American publisher, Stanley H. Barkan, organised a six week poetry reading tour for Peter and Dylan Thomas's daughter, Aeronwy. The pair gave readings and workshops from New York to California, at many universities and prestigious art venues.

Peter is also the co-author, with Aeronwy, of the *Dylan Thomas Walking Tour of Greenwich Village*. He was invited to Serbia in 2006 by the Serbian Writers' Association to participate in the 43rd International Meeting of Writers in Belgrade. He was visiting poet in Romania in 2008 and 2009, where he carried out readings and poetry workshops at colleges and universities.

He is the recipient of the Eric Gregory Award for Poetry (The Society of Authors, London), The Society of Authors Award, The Royal Literary Fund Award (London) and an Arts Council of Wales Award. He has been a prize-winner in several UK and international poetry competitions.

He resided at Big Sur, California, in 2010 as writer-in-residence, returning again for a second and third residency in 2011 and 2012. Whilst in California in 2012, Peter wrote the drama about Big Sur sculptor Edmund Kara, who is famous for his sculpture of Elizabeth Taylor in the film *The Sandpiper*.

Peter is the Founder and Editor of *The Seventh Quarry Swansea Poetry Magazine*, which publishes poetry, translations and articles from around the world, and the accompanying The Seventh Quarry Publishing Press, which publishes international books of poetry, prose, and art.

His poem "Kilvey Hill" has been incorporated into a permanent stained-glass window at Saint Thomas Community School in Swansea, Wales.

Peter has participated in many festivals and conferences in America and Europe, including World Affairs Conference, Colorado, 2009; NEMLA Conferences, (Boston, 2013, Pennsylvania, 2014, and Toronto, 2015); and the Massachusetts Poetry Festival. He has also organized A Visiting American Students/Dylan Thomas in Wales Project with Knox College, America, 2010, and an International Poetry Festival, 2011, and a Drama Festival, 2012, at the Dylan Thomas Theatre, Swansea, Wales. The latter two events were a collaboration with Cross-Cultural Communications, New York.

In December 2012, Peter was one of just eight people invited to meet His Royal Highness Prince Charles at the Dylan Thomas Birthplace in Swansea.

He returned to California, as a writer-in-residence, in the summer of 2013 and 2014. In 2014, he was a participant in a number of DT100 events in the UK and in America celebrating the Centenary of the birth of Dylan Thomas. The *Dylan Thomas Walking Tour of Greenwich Village, New York* book and smartphone app were launched by the Right Honourable Carwyn Jones, the First Minister of Wales, accompanied by Peter and Hannah Ellis, Dylan's granddaughter, in New York. Peter was also the co-organiser of a Dylan Thomas Multilingual/International Creative Writing Competition and the organiser of a Dylan Thomas Centenary Quotations Trail at the National Waterfront Museum, Swansea.

His short drama, *The Poet, the Hunchback, and The Boy,* based on the poem 'The hunchback in the park' by Dylan Thomas, is available as a DVD, as part of the Centenary celebrations of the Dylan Thomas Theatre, Swansea. The drama was performed by Theatre actors at the National Waterfront Museum, Swansea, and The Welsh Centre, London, in May 2013.

Two chapters of a book of literary criticism by Professor Alexandru Zotto, a leading critic, are devoted to Peter's poetry and drama in a book, INTERMINTENTE/CRITICE III/ESEURU DESPRE POEZIE, published by Citadela Publishing, Romania.

In April, 2014, he was inducted into the Phi Sigma Iota Society at Salem State University, Massachusetts, for his contribution to literature and literary translations.

Peter returned to Big Sur, California, in 2015 and 2016 as writer-in-residence.

He was awarded the Ted Slade Award for Service to Poetry in 2016 by The Poetry Kit, UK.

Further information: www.peterthabitjones.com

SOME COMMENTS ON OTHER BOOKS BY PETER THABIT JONES

What we have here, in these poems of sonic-semantic summation, is a physical/spiritual assertion and acceptance, as if in a genuflection gesture, of Life's Enigma, its simultaneity of birth and ultimate death . . . And it is all here in such a volume of verse, the poet, Peter, as wordsmith, as visionary vessel of faith, as "being is believing:" the poem, always this ideal cage of form, of braiding of selves, of the very sea surge that is Life's sacrosanct Enigma.

   —**American Emeritus Professor Vince Clemente, from his introduction to Poems from a Cabin on Big Sur**

It is not Jones's subject matter alone that makes him a strong poet and his work exemplary. He is an extraordinary poet because he understands, and utilizes, devices and techniques many poets today downplay or discard entirely: namely, rhyme (both external and internal) and meter . . . At times joyous and at times melancholy, The Lizard Catchers is an excellent new collection from one of Wales's premier poets. Not only for fans of world literature (and literature from the United Kingdom, in particular), it is also a desirable collection for any reader who appreciates well-crafted language and the skilful employment of traditional techniques.

   —**Joselle Vanderhooft, from her review of The Lizard Catchers in The Pedestal Magazine (USA)**

With his wide range of subject matter and his dynamic way of representing intense emotions, his beautifully crafted poems engage us in the real world. There is a selection of poems for children towards the end of the book, all lively and concise, including the emotive 'Some people in other lands'. Overall, this is an intelligent and interesting collection of poems – definitely to be opened often.

> **—Clare Maynard, Welsh Books Council/Gwales.com, from her review of The Lizard Catchers (With the permission of the Welsh Books Council)**

It made an incredible impact on the audiences during the first Dylan Thomas Tribute Tour of America, Spring 2008, since the death of Dylan in 1953. Peter Thabit Jones has been established as a poet of stones and sunshine, a remarkable synthesis, which both inspires and enlightens, a new powerful, humanistic voice from Wales.

> **—AMAZON.COM from a review of The Lizard Catchers**

I must say, I have never read anything like this: seemingly random human assertions, lamentations, spontaneous chants; yet the verse drama remains seamless in its verbal texture, in its balanced, often antiphonal metrical design. Nothing is wasted. Every call or cry or meditation in this "poem for five characters" is heard, come to settle in a grateful reader, forever there, in the larder of the heart.

> **—American Emeritus Professor Vince Clemente, from his introduction to The Boy and The Lion's Head, a verse drama**

The great art of the poet consists in the introduction of those daily elements by which he brings the Boy closer to us. The war, for instance, obsessively recurs because nothing more absurd has ever been invented by man! In a word, I have read a poem that can be performed by each of us. Because each of us covers this way of initiation. Peter Thabit Jones opens the horizon to Kilvey Hill for us, describing by the quasi-totality of the poetic techniques the way he has taken himself to solve the world enigma that is life.

> **—Liviu Comşia (Romania), from her review of The Boy and the Lion's Head, a verse drama**

The coherence and cohesion of this poem is also reached with the help of the space unity, the continuity and the recurrence of the moments and the existential acts, the familial structure of the characters, all supporting, together with the oracular uttering and the metaphoric language and the ritualization of life. By this aesthetic effect the concrete aspects of everyday life intensify and amplify their functions making the ordinary fact reach significances with destiny value.

—Professor Alexandru Zotta (Romania), from his review of The Boy and the Lion's Head, a verse drama